End

David Eldridge

methuen | drama

LONDON • NEW YORK • OXFORD • NEW DELHI • SYDNEY

METHUEN DRAMA

Bloomsbury Publishing Plc, 50 Bedford Square, London, WC1B 3DP, UK
Bloomsbury Publishing Inc, 1359 Broadway, New York, NY 10018, USA
Bloomsbury Publishing Ireland, 29 Earlsfort Terrace, Dublin 2, D02 AY28, Ireland

BLOOMSBURY, METHUEN DRAMA and the Methuen
Drama logo are trademarks of Bloomsbury Publishing Plc

First published in Great Britain 2025

Copyright © David Eldridge, 2025

David Eldridge has asserted his right under the Copyright, Designs
and Patents Act, 1988, to be identified as author of this work.

Cover design by Megan Wilson
Cover photo © Ana Lui via Getty Images

All rights reserved. No part of this publication may be: i) reproduced or transmitted in
any form, electronic or mechanical, including photocopying, recording or by means of
any information storage or retrieval system without prior permission in writing from
the publishers; or ii) used or reproduced in any way for the training, development or
operation of artificial intelligence (AI) technologies, including generative AI technologies.
The rights holders expressly reserve this publication from the text and data mining
exception as per Article 4(3) of the Digital Single Market Directive (EU) 2019/790.

Bloomsbury Publishing Plc does not have any control over, or responsibility for,
any third-party websites referred to or in this book. All internet addresses given in this
book were correct at the time of going to press. The author and publisher regret
any inconvenience caused if addresses have changed or sites have ceased
to exist, but can accept no responsibility for any such changes.

No rights in incidental music or songs contained in the work are hereby granted
and performance rights for any performance/presentation whatsoever
must be obtained from the respective copyright owners.

All rights whatsoever in this play are strictly reserved and application for performance
etc. should be made before rehearsals by professionals and by amateurs to
Independent Talent, 40 Whitfield Street, London, W1T 2RH, UK.
No performance may be given unless a licence has been obtained.

A catalogue record for this book is available from the British Library.

A catalog record for this book is available from the Library of Congress.

ISBN:	PB:	978-1-3506-0938-9
	ePDF:	978-1-3506-0939-6
	eBook:	978-1-3506-0940-2

Series: Modern Plays

Typeset by Westchester Publishing Services
Printed and bound in Great Britain

For product safety related questions contact productsafety@bloomsbury.com.

To find out more about our authors and books visit
www.bloomsbury.com and sign up for our newsletters.

End

David Eldridge

The Company

Cast, in alphabetical order

Alfie	**Clive Owen**
Julie	**Saskia Reeves**

Director	**Rachel O'Riordan**
Set and Costume Designer	**Gary McCann**
Lighting Designer	**Sally Ferguson**
Sound Designer	**Donato Wharton**
Intimacy Director	**Bethan Clark**
Casting	**Alastair Coomer CDG**
Voice Coach	**Cathleen McCarron**
Dialect Coach	**Patricia Logue**
Associate Sound Designer	**Nick Mann**
Staff Director	**Philip J Morris**

Producer	**Adwoa-Alexsis Mintah**
Production Manager	**Kate Chapman**
Dramaturg	**Clare Slater**
Company Stage Manager	**Ben Donoghue**
Deputy Stage Manager	**Caoimhe Regan**
Assistant Stage Manager	**Ellie Penney (DSM Cover)**
Stage Management Cover	**Fana Sunley-Smith**
Project Draughting	**Gemma Grosvenor**
Digital Art	**Daniel Radley-Bennett**
Costume Supervisor	**Male Arcucci**
Wigs, Hair & Make-up Supervisor	**Daisy Beer**
Running Wardrobe Supervisor	**Bethan Kelly**
Props Supervisor	**Chris Lake**
Props Buyer	**Kinga Czynciel**
Props Making Coordinator	**Annie Lumby**
Lighting Supervisor	**Matt Harding**

Lead Lighting Programmer	**Will Frost**
Assistant Lighting Programmer	**Max Cherry**
Production Sound Engineer	**Claire Carroll**
Sound Operator	**Molly Barron**
Radio Mic Supervisor	**Clio Nonis**
Stage Supervisor	**Lee Harrington**
Rigging Supervisor	**James 'Luka' Goodsall**
Construction Supervisor	**Sam Stacey**
Scenic Art Supervisor	**Alice Collie**
Production Photographer	**Marc Brenner**

The National Theatre's workshops are responsible for, on this production: armoury; costume; props & furniture; scenic art; scenic construction; scenic lighting; sound & video; wigs, hair & make-up.

Opening
Dorfman Theatre, 20 November 2025

Please note, this version went to press before the first performance and so the script may differ slightly from the final performance.

End

For Mum & For Robert

This play takes place in a real room and in real time – but stage directions are indicative not prescriptive. This play is the third of a loose trilogy of plays – or triptych – for the theatre.

Thanks to Caroline Winder, Michael McCoy, Rachel O'Riordan, Saskia Reeves, Clive Owen, Polly Findlay, Rufus Norris, Clare Slater, Nina Steiger, Justine Mitchell & Peter Sullivan.

And special thanks to Fatboy Slim & Terry Farley; Professor Daniel Hochhauser, Mr Manish Chand & Dr Kai-Keen Shiu; and to Daragh Carville & Julia Bell.

Mid-June, 2016

The lounge diner of a large terraced house in Harringay, London.

At the lounge end is a sofa. There's a blanket and a pillow on the sofa. At the other end is a dining table.

A window is open and the sound of a little birdsong finds its way into the room. There's a large serving hatch and you can see into the kitchen. The clock on the kitchen wall says ten to seven in the morning.

There are lots of books and the room has a great but discreet audio sound system.

There's an open door leading out towards the hallway, leading to the kitchen and the stairs. Not that we see the whole house but it's big. There are four bedrooms, the loft has been converted and there's a studio at the end of the garden.

Alfie, *58, is standing with the aid of a medical walking stick. He's in an expensive hoodie, a bit too young for him, 2013/14 West Ham home shorts and some Adidas sliders. His medication has taken the edge off his pain.*

His wife, **Julie**, *58, looks at him. She's in a pretty summer dress with pockets, a bit too young for her, too. She has some clothes for* **Alfie** *over her right arm.*

Alfie *finally turns and looks at* **Julie**.

They look at each other for as long as you think you can get away with.

Alfie   I love you darling.

Julie   I love you too.

Alfie   I've accepted what Dr Chan said on Friday.

Julie   Okay.

Alfie   And I've decided I don't want any more treatment.

Julie What?

Silence.

Alfie I know Mr Rahman thinks I've made the right decision.

Silence.

Julie Have you taken your tablets?

Alfie *nods.* **Julie** *puts down* **Alfie**'s *clothes on the sofa and goes to him.*

They hold each other for a long time, just hold each other. They look at each other, kiss, look at each other again.

Alfie I'll be okay. Are you?

Julie I'm okay.

Alfie What time's Annabelle coming?

Julie About half past eight. Nine.

Alfie Will you help me talk to her?

Silence.

Alfie Is Toby coming?

Julie No he's on that stag do. I did say.

Alfie Yeah. Sorry.

Julie He's coming back this afternoon.

Alfie My memory sometimes.

Julie *heads towards the kitchen, stops, turns.*

Julie You don't think Toby would do anything . . .

Alfie What?

Julie You know . . . With his mates. In Amsterdam.

Alfie What?

Julie Annabelle's convinced herself he's up to all sorts with his mates.

Alfie Like what?

Julie You know . . . With a window girl . . .

Alfie How do you know what they're called?

Julie Everyone knows what they're called.

Alfie I'm pulling your leg! Toby probably had a few pints. Went in a coffee shop for a smoke with his mates. Went back to the hotel early and spent the rest of the night with his head down a toilet. That kid can't take his drink. Oh, Ju, I'd give my fucking right bollock. For two days on the turps in Amsterdam . . .

Julie I know, Espresso martini, cheeky little livener and a big fat doobie.

Alfie I'd give both my bollocks. Shrooms. Bosh. A pill. A club. Hair of the dog. Bosh.

Julie *laughs. Silence.*

Julie I think Annabelle said all the lads are in apartments. I bet they're having a right old laugh . . .

Alfie Does it matter?

Julie What?

Alfie Does it matter whether they're in a hotel or apartments?

Julie I was only saying. Chill your boots. Annabelle doesn't like the idea of him being on the stag do with his mates.

Alfie Why?

Julie You know what she's like, she's so serious about everything, Alf . . . I don't know what planet she's on, he's nearly as square as she is . . .

Alfie How on earth did we manage to give birth to Annabelle?

Julie Ahem, I think you'll find it was me that gave birth to her, Alf...

Alfie Are you sure there wasn't a moment of passion with Boring Tone when I wasn't looking?

Julie Oh God I've not thought about him in years, what a nerk...

Alfie Boring Tone was so boring after speaking to him I needed a lie down for three days...

Julie Boring Tone was so boring he used to make me paranoid it was contagious...

Alfie *laughs, thinks.*

Alfie Love her dearly though I do, I cannot fathom how us two managed to bring into being Saffy two-point-zero. Go on, break my heart...

Julie I've never done anything like that. Have I? Dickhead.

Alfie *laughs. Silence.*

Julie I think with Toby she can see herself settling down properly.

Alfie Can she?

Julie Alf! Have you been living under a rock?

Alfie As far as I'm concerned it's off and then it's on. It's off and then it's on...

Julie She trusts him. But she's realising how much she likes him. She feels insecure at the same time.

Alfie The absolute worst Toby will have done is have a little smoke and have a little puke and maybe been to see a sex show...

Julie Imagine Annabelle's face?

Alfie I know.

Julie She doesn't honestly think Toby and his mates have gone to Amsterdam to pick her some tulips and look at a painting of a Milkmaid?

Alfie *laughs. Silence.*

Julie I think she had a right old set to with Toby on Friday morning before he went. Don't get annoyed, I've not said . . . But she's been seeing her counsellor again, Alf. Her anxiety's going through the roof.

Alfie You should have told me that . . .

Julie Didn't you try and protect your dad from things? When he was ill.

Silence.

Julie She wants us all to be together this morning. She wants some mummy and daddy love and a bacon sandwich.

Silence.

Julie I don't know how you're going to explain all this to Annabelle. She'll want you to chuck the kitchen sink at it.

Alfie For another year? At best.

Silence.

Alfie And what about you, babe?

Julie What about me?

Alfie How are you?

Julie Don't worry about me, Alf.

Silence.

Alfie Do you wish we'd got married?

Julie No. I'm happy as I am.

Alfie Really?

Julie I mean, I'm not happy you're not well . . .

Alfie It's okay.

Julie We've had a wonderful life. I've been so happy.

Alfie Have we?

Julie I think so. Don't you?

Alfie There's other things I want, Ju.

Julie Like what?

Alfie You heard what Dr Chan said. You didn't let go of my hand once. If I stop. Three months. We've got to get things straight. We've got be on the same page here, babe, haven't we?

Julie Right, tea.

Alfie Annabelle's got nothing to worry about with Toby. He's a good kid.

Julie When did you go and see a sex show?

Alfie It was donkeys' years ago. It was on the wind-down after 'Dance Valley'.

Julie Right.

Alfie It was nothing, Ju. What's up? You're never weird about this stuff . . .

Julie I was only asking a question.

Alfie Do you think we'll ever have sex again?

Julie I beg your pardon?

Alfie Do you think we'll ever make love again?

Julie What's all this about now?

Alfie I love you darling.

Julie Of course we will.

Alfie I wonder if we will though?

Silence.

Julie Were you alright coming down?

Alfie I was fine.

Julie I had my heart in my mouth.

Alfie I came down on my bum.

Julie Have you been listening to music?

Alfie Yeah I.

Julie Okay.

Alfie Yeah I want to choose the record.

Julie What for?

Alfie Maybe a couple of records.

Julie Right?

Alfie You know what for.

Julie I don't, Alf.

Alfie For the service.

Julie What, at half past six in the morning?

Alfie Darling, I've spent my whole adult life playing records at half past six in the morning.

Julie *laughs, so does* **Alfie**. *Silence.*

Julie Do you want some tea?

Alfie No.

Julie Shall I make a pot of coffee?

Alfie No, I don't fancy it.

Julie Did you pick one?

Alfie I kind of went down a rabbit hole. I mean obviously. My heart was exploding.

10 End

Alfie *fishes his iPhone out of his hoodie pocket, selects the Apple Music app, finds the song and presses play. 'Going Back to My Roots' by Richie Havens plays.*

Alfie I think this tune's a contender.

Alfie *watches* **Julie** *intently, she takes a breath to steady herself, listens. Almost immediately he switches it off.*

Julie It's okay.

Alfie It's alright. Annabelle's coming.

Julie No go on, I want you to.

Alfie Look, we can do it another time . . .

Julie So what are you thinking?

Alfie Erm.

Julie When do you want them played? Go on. It's okay.

Alfie I haven't had a chance to think it through properly.

Julie Okay.

Alfie We haven't talked about it, have we, Ju? We got to, Ju.

Julie Well let's talk.

Alfie You and Annabelle. Music-a. It's been my life.

Julie I know, love.

Julie *moves to go to him but hesitates, catching the look on his face.*

Alfie It's alright.

Julie Let me.

Alfie If we . . . I won't. I can't.

Julie Go on, love.

Alfie I want a good end.

They look at each other for as long as you think you can get away with.

They both use all their willpower and courage to stay present in the room.

Alfie *looks at his iPhone and back at* **Julie**.

Julie It's okay. It's not okay. But it's okay.

Alfie Really I want a record to play as they carry me out at the end of the service. One of my favourites, Ju. I don't want any of that John Lennon 'Imagine' bollocks.

Alfie *finds another song and presses play.*

'Total Confusion' by A Homeboy, A Hippie & A Funki Dredd & The Future Sound of London plays.

They listen to a bit. **Alfie** *nods his head.* **Julie** *is horrified.* **Alfie** *switches it off and beams at her.*

Julie You want that?

Alfie Babe, joke. Joke, babe.

Alfie *laughs his head off and so does* **Julie** *a bit, with relief.*

Julie Prick.

Alfie Always, babe, always been a dickhead.

Julie Fucking prick, honestly.

Alfie Alright, don't rub it in.

They laugh.

Alfie I want to give people a lift at the end. You've got to finish your set with a banger.

Alfie *finds another song and presses play on his iPhone.*

'Lady (Hear Me Tonight)' by Modjo plays. They listen to a bit, look at each other.

Julie I like this one.

They both nod their heads and **Julie** *dicks about a bit.* **Alfie** *switches it off. Silence.*

12   End

Alfie   I feel so young.

Julie   I know. I always want to dance when I hear this one. I always used to like coming down when it was you and Julius and Tall Paul.

Alfie   It was nice. Romain Tranchart put the Acetate in my hand. And I thought fuck it. I put it on the slip mat. And had a little listen. And there's that Chic Nile Rogers guitar. And I'm like let's do it. Let's do it. Let's do it. Ministry exploded. It went off.

Julie   I bet.

Alfie   It's hard ain't it?

Julie   Yeah. Really hard.

Alfie   I'm thinking about Mum. Singing in the kitchen. Peeling the potatoes. And Nan. Mum and Nan thick as thieves. In the Pie and Mash. Mum eating jellied eels and Nan eating stewed eels. Mug of tea and false teeth on the table. And Mum and Dad dancing in the sitting room on a Sunday. Mum playing her seven-inch singles. Motown and Atlantic. Me and Dad dicking around singing 'I'm Forever Blowing Bubbles'. Shall we park all this until later?

Julie   I'm alright, Alf.

Alfie   You sure, Ju?

Julie   What's on your mind?

Alfie   He's nice that Dr Chan.

Julie   It's hard to accept, Alfie.

Alfie   Got a nice way about him.

Julie   Would you accept it? If it was me?

Alfie   I'm sure I wouldn't. If the boot was on the other foot I daresay I'd want you to chuck the kitchen sink at it.

Julie Well then. We've got be on the same page on this one haven't we, babe?

Alfie We have.

Julie Go on, spit it out.

Alfie I want to go home. I want to be with Mum and Dad. And Nan. Up at London Road cemetery. I know we've lived here a long time now, babe. I know I've done a thing or two in my life but I don't want to be in Highgate Cemetery. With Karl Marx and Malcolm-fucking-McLaren.

Silence.

Alfie I'm from Collier Row. I'm an Essex Boy. I don't know no one there.

Julie Okay we can go there. When the time comes we can be laid to rest together there.

Alfie I want to be in with my mum and my dad. And my nan. I don't want to be on my own.

Julie But I thought we'd be together?

Julie *wants to cry, doesn't.*

Alfie What?

Julie I thought, not for a long, long time. But. Like. I've had this notion. It's got me by.

Julie *exercises all her willpower so she doesn't cry.*

Alfie When the time comes you can be with me up at Brentwood . . .

Julie What your mum and your dad and your nan – and me and you – all in together?

Alfie Yeah.

Julie You can only put four in one plot. Your mum didn't like me, Alf.

Alfie Don't be like that.

Julie It's alright. You've told me now. I'm fine with it. It doesn't matter.

Alfie Go on. I'm all ears.

Julie I've been trying to block a lot out. But when I have. You know?

Alfie Yeah.

Julie I've been telling myself this story. Walking over, over Harringay Station, through Crouch End. And over Suicide Bridge. Stopping for some flowers on Highgate Hill. Ambling through Waterlow Park. I've always loved Waterlow Park. Looking at the city. The Shard on the tree line. Then coming to see you. A headstone of a carved book. You on the left page and some space for me on the right. And the words. Our words. 'I have loved thee with an everlasting love.'

Alfie That's all gone through your mind? Is there any chance I could have some engravings as well?

Julie Engravings? Like what?

Alfie A Twelve Hundred. And a glitterball. And a smoke machine. With a little strawberry tab. So everyone knows it's the same flavour as the one Danny had at Shoom.

Julie Right?

Alfie And maybe perched on the arm of the turntable. A Hammerette in a low-cut top. Showing a bit of tit. Look class that on a gravestone.

Alfie *pulls a face.*

Julie You are such a dickhead. You're such a fucking cock.

Alfie *laughs, so does* **Julie**.

Alfie 'I have loved thee with an everlasting love.' Is that it? Is that the words?

Julie Yeah.

Alfie That's so beautiful. You should be a writer.

Julie   Fuck off.

Alfie   I'm proud of you. You know I am.

Julie   Shall we have some tea? Alf?

Alfie   I am. I was so proud of you when your book came out. I've been proud of all of them. Every single one.

Julie   Alfie it's such a pain to get from Harringay to the cemetery in Brentwood.

Alfie   Ju . . .

Julie   When I want to come and see you I've either got to drive. Or I've got to get the chugga-chugga to Wanstead Park, walk down to Forest Gate and come back out again . . . For Christ's sake, Alf. It's not going to be you is it, on your birthday? Or Christmas? I've never begrudged you anything have I, babe?

Alfie   No, I'll be having a nice long kip in the ground. It's what I want, Ju.

Julie   Honestly, I'll have you excavated and moved in the middle of the night!

Alfie   No! You can't do that!

They both laugh.

Julie   Well you've got it off your chest now. I'm glad you've said what you wanted to say.

Alfie   I haven't.

Julie   What?

Alfie   I haven't said what I wanted to say.

Julie   What there's more?

They look at each other for as long as you think you can get away with.

Alfie   The thing I find really overwhelming. The thing I find really hard.

16 End

Julie Go on.

Alfie I'm not actually scared of going. I know I'll just go to sleep in the end. That's all it is. I just won't wake up.

Silence.

Julie Go on, you can do it. You can say it.

Alfie It's the before.

Julie What do you mean?

Alfie You know what it was like with Dad. About a week before he went. And he had all of his marbles. And we talked. Every time I said goodbye. I said 'Bye, Dad. See you tomorrow. I love you, Dad'. And we never ever said I love you, did we?

Julie No.

Alfie And he'd make a joke of it. 'I love you boy. Go on fuck off home. I'll see you tomorrow.'

Julie *laughs.*

Alfie I always turned round to look at him one last time before I went out of his room. And I could see in his eyes. And he could see in my eyes. In my whole demeanour. It's like. How many more times are we going look each other? Is this it?

Silence.

Alfie You know? How many more times will I come round the North Circular and drop off on to the Chigwell Road. Up through Collier Row. And all those thoughts of being boy. Of the view from Lawns Park. The city. London. Where I knew I always wanted to be. Just before I went down the hill on my sledge. You know? Make a right into Broxhill Road and then a sharp left into St Francis's. Again. Is he here? Is he still with us? He's still here. Running out of puff. I go in to his room. I kiss him. Smell him. Dad. The smell of his hair. Dad. We look at each other. The relief. In both of us. Last time wasn't the last time.

Silence.

Alfie That feeling. Strangely euphoric. It's gone right away. Fuck. This is it. This is the last time. The hurt. I don't want that.

Alfie *gathers himself, closes his eyes, uses all his strength to stay composed.*

Julie What do you mean, darling?

Alfie When I was boy playing in the garden. I saw a snake. It was a summer's morning. Like this morning. And I was in the garden. I was terrified. I properly shit myself. I would have been eight. That's it. It was. The summer West Ham won the World Cup . . .

Julie Honestly . . .

Alfie What?

Julie How many times have I heard that shit joke?

Alfie *laughs.* **Julie** *laughs.*

Alfie It must have been the first time in my life. I'd had the conscious thought 'I'm going to die'. Then Dad put his hand on my shoulder. And he said 'It's only an old English grass snake, boy. He won't bite. He's not interested in you. Now, an adder. He's a different kettle of fish. He might bite. But you'll know how to spot him. Because he's got a zig-zag pattern down his back. And he's got red eyes.' I said, 'red eyes?' He said 'Yes son, red eyes, like the devil'. I said 'I don't want to play in the garden anymore'. And when I was that age I spent all summer in the garden. And you know what Dad said? He said, 'Son, I tell you what I'm going to do. I'm going to go in my toolbox and get you my hammer. The big one. And you if you see an adder. You give him a great big fucking whack on the head'.

Alfie *laughs.* **Julie** *laughs.*

Alfie When I was a kid the six weeks summer holiday felt like it was endless. And then it was August bank holiday. Mum and Dad screaming and shouting about the cost of my new school uniform. And then one day it starts to rain.

Julie How come you've never told me that story?

Alfie I didn't want you to put it in a book.

Julie What?

Silence.

Alfie I've not thought about it in years. I've been thinking about all sorts of things this morning. Romford's become part of London. But when we was kids, it was separate. It was Essex. Wasn't it, darling?

Julie What are you saying all this for, Alf?

Alfie Once I'm ready to be moved in to St John's. Or the North London. Wherever they can fit me in. I want us all to be together for one last time. You, Annabelle. Toby if Annabelle wants him there. And I want to say goodbye properly to everyone. And know when I've got all my wits about me. This is it. This is the end for us. And we know. We know where we are. Everyone knows if you don't say this. Or that. Now. That's it.

Julie We? What you saying, Alf?

Alfie Once I've gone into the hospice I want to be on my own.

Julie *covers her mouth involuntarily. Silence.*

Alfie I thought maybe this next one. When they bring me in. In to the church.

Alfie *finds another song and presses play on his iPhone.*

'My Lover's Prayer' by Otis Redding plays. They listen to a bit, look at each other.

Julie Alfie –

Alfie *immediately switches it off.*

Alfie I associate it with Mum. She loved soul music. Loved a crooner. Sam Cooke. Nat King Cole. Otis.

Julie I know.

Alfie I've kind of got this mad idea. You know? Of it playing. And it's like. I'm coming home, Mum.

Julie Alf –

Alfie I want to be buried in my Chipie dungarees and my Kickers.

Julie What?

Alfie It's all in that vacuum pack in the loft. It'll all fit me again now . . .

Julie Alf, babe . . .

Alfie I don't even know why I'm even saying all this. I don't want a funeral.

Julie You what?

Alfie I don't like the idea. I want to say goodbye while I've got all my wits about me. And I'm not too weak. And that's it. Throw a party a month or two later. I'm sure one of my mates will play some records.

Julie Don't you want me to hold your hand? Don't you think I want to hold your hand?

Alfie I can't think of anything worse than us fading out. Me all drugged up. Except maybe I can still hear a bit. The sound of you and Annabelle. Crying.

Julie We won't.

Alfie Hearing you suffering.

Julie I promise you we won't. We're strong, babe, we're strong.

Alfie It's my worst fear.

Julie I will give you everything to comfort you. And calm you. And love you.

Alfie I'd rather be on my own at the End.

Julie This isn't right, Alf. What about me and Annabelle? What about me and Annabelle?

Alfie It's best for all of us.

Julie It's not.

Alfie It is.

Julie You're only thinking of one person here. And it's not me and it's not Annabelle.

Alfie I know I don't deserve you.

Julie Why are you doing this?

Silence.

Julie The night we got together in Daniels. You said 'do you believe in love at first sight?' And I said, yes. And you got hold of my hand. And you said. That's it now, babe. I'm never letting go . . .

Alfie What a nutty little club.

Julie You looked so pure.

Alfie Baby face.

Julie And I had no idea you were such a thug when you went to football.

Alfie I can't think of anything lonelier. Than watching you, watching me go. The last things I hear is your voice quivering. Like it does when I know that great big heart's gonna break. We'll be together again one day.

Julie We won't. Don't talk nonsense, Alf. This is it.

Silence.

Julie I've known you since I was twenty-three years of age. And we haven't had no religious crap once. Don't start now. This is it.

Alfie Please, Julie.

Julie What about me? What about Annabelle? For crying out loud, Alfie. There's something going on here. I'm not stupid.

Julie *goes into the kitchen and boils the kettle.*

She makes a pot of tea and brings it in, finding a heatproof mat before she puts it on the dining table.

It's an elegant old china teapot, at odds with the rest of their taste.

Alfie I'm glad me and Annabelle got over to West Ham to see the last one.

Julie It meant a lot to her.

Alfie I wish we'd gone to football together a bit more often.

Julie She enjoyed going over with you when she went.

Alfie It's hard to believe this time next year we'll have done our first season in the Olympic stadium. It was so depressing when Man U went two-one up. It was like, this is so West Ham. There's gonna be no happy ending here.

Julie No.

Alfie And then. Bosh. Payet floats it in and Michail Antonio's up like a salmon. And it's in the net. Goal. Quarter of an hour to go. Valencia concedes the free kick. It's Payet again.

Perfect. Winston Reid. He's not up like a salmon.

Julie *laughs.*

Alfie But he gets his nut on it. Goal!

Alfie *celebrates like a Brazilian football commentator, waving his walking stick in the air.*

Alfie GOOOOOOOOOOOOOOOOOAAAAAAAAAAA AAAAAAAAAAAALLLLLLL! GOOOOOOOOOOOAAA AAAAAAAAAAALLLLLLLLLLLLLLLLLLLLLLLLL! WINSTON-REIIIIIIIIIIIIIIIIIIIIIIIIIIIIIIIIIIIIIIID! WINNNNNNNNNNNSTON REID GOOOOOOOO OOOOOOOAAAAAAAAAAAAAAAAAALLLLLLLLLLL! BELO! BELO! BELO!

Alfie *laughs,* **Julie** *laughs.*

Julie Do you really want to be on your own?

Silence.

Alfie Ten minutes to go. Kouyaté has a pop. Five minutes go. Ref checks his watch. Five minutes on the board. Another five minutes. We're all whistling. Come on, ref! And then he blows up. He blows up. We've done Man U. We've won. We've won. Our last ever game at Upton Park. Everyone was going nuts. And me and Annabelle are hanging onto each other for dear life. Laughing and crying. Laughing and crying. When we walked up Green Street towards the tube. She held my hand like she was eight years old again. It's funny to think it was the last time we'll ever do that. Somehow knowing it was the last time for everyone takes the edge off. I do understand what it is I'm asking.

Julie I don't know what Annabelle's going to say.

Silence.

Alfie It's a bit weird to think we'll be in the Olympic Stadium next season and I won't be going.

Julie I reckon you'll be alright to go to the first one.

Alfie I won't. I'll be on the way out by then.

Julie I loved the Olympics.

Alfie I'll never forget Mo winning that ten thousand metres.

Julie It was magic.

Alfie That little look over his shoulder. Just to make sure.

Julie I've been thinking of writing a novel set over that summer.

Alfie Have you, babe?

Julie Yeah, yeah, I've been thinking about for a while.

Alfie Great.

Julie It's been a bit hard to commit to it. You know? While there's been so much uncertainty.

Alfie I'm sorry.

Julie It's not your fault.

Alfie I sometimes feel like it is.

Julie It's not.

Alfie I've not exactly had the healthiest lifestyle.

Julie It's just cancer. The cunt.

Silence.

Alfie Have you got a story?

Julie I like that Michael Cunningham novel. The one that was turned into a film. The one that was riffing off *Mrs Dalloway*.

Alfie You thinking of doing something a bit more arty?

Julie The thought of writing another crime book actually bores me to tears.

Alfie You go for it, darling.

Julie I think I'm going to write under a different name.

Alfie Really?

Julie Yeah. I can't put that novel out under my name. I'm in a box with Martina Cole as it is. I'll be patronised to fuck.

Alfie What is it?

Julie What? The novel?

Alfie Yeah.

Julie Ordinary people. Little earthquakes in their lives. The opening ceremony. The hundred metres final. The closing ceremony. I'm imagining it's quite stream of consciousness. I really want to write like that. Write normal people like us. Like that. My agent's going to lose her shit. All she'll be able to see is me flushing pound notes down the toilet.

Alfie Don't worry about her . . .

Julie She'll be alright. She'll have to be.

Alfie What's your pen name then?

Julie I was thinking Olivia du Grosseins. Pronounced Grosseins.

Alfie Olivia du Grosseins?

Julie What?

Alfie Olivia du Grosseins?

Julie Yeah?

Alfie What's with the French angle, Ju?

Julie I thought you had a CSE in French?

Alfie 'Mange tout, Julie, mange tout'.

Julie Are you taking the piss?

Alfie I can only apologise darling for being such an ignoramus . . .

Julie It's French for 'big breasts'.

Alfie Big what?

Julie Olivia du Big Breasts. *Sunday Times* bestseller and a Hollywood option.

Julie *laughs and gradually* **Alfie** *laughs. They set each other off. They both laugh until they cry.*

Alfie It's a long time since we've been ordinary people.

Julie Where you're from never leaves you. Not really. Does it, Alf?

Alfie Perhaps you'll get going on your book before Christmas?

Julie There's another book I want to do first.

Alfie Blimey, what's that one? There's another one?

Silence.

Julie I loved that the summer. The Olympics. Everything felt so hopeful.

Alfie Will you do what I want?

Julie Don't you think we need a new approach, Alf? Maybe we need to look abroad. Go down a more integrative route . . .

Alfie Abroad where?

Julie I know the chemo's brutal so maybe we need something less toxic . . .

Alfie Like what?

Julie I've been looking and looking and looking on Google and there's a whole world out there. It goes far beyond what Dr Chan and Mr Rahman have put on the table, babe.

These people abroad. They harness the power existing inside all of us. That's inside our bodies already. It's Metabolic, Alf. You detoxify. They strengthen your immune system. And then they go after the cancer with organic, natural chemicals. The drug's called Laetrile. There's this clinic I've found that'll suit us down to the ground.

Alfie And how much is all this going to cost?

Julie Fifty grand. Ish.

Alfie Fifty grand?

Julie That's what our rainy day money's for, Alfie.

Alfie That's for Annabelle when we're gone . . .

Julie Annabelle will want her dad to be around.

Alfie Where is it?

Julie Tijuana.

Alfie Tijuana?

Julie Yeah.

Alfie The last time I went to Tijuana I was held hostage for twelve hours by a Cartel who had a beef with the promoter of the rave. I had all me records nicked and I never got paid. No thanks, babe.

Julie These people are curing people. Their scans are clean Alf. We've got so much more to come.

Silence.

Julie Year after next we've both got our big birthday, haven't we? The big six-o. That is our year, babe. We've got to get you well. We've got to have our party. The Earl Haig in Crouch End. That's perfect that is. They'll let us have the whole place to ourselves. Get one hundred and fifty in there easy. We'll have a really good do. And we've got to go on our holidays. It's always been a dream of mine since I was a little girl to go to Hawaii.

Waikiki Beach and a little bit of Hula-Hula. And I know you want to walk the Dolomites.

Alfie Walk the Dolomites?

Julie All the beautiful meadows of the South Tyrol. The Lake at Misurina. Lunch at the Larieto.

Alfie I could no more walk the Dolomites than I could walk down to Green Lanes to nip into Tesco.

Julie There'll come a day when we're both thinning out so much on top we'll cut our hair. Start looking the same.

Matching gilets. And a National Trust membership. Pottering round Chartwell. Holding hands. And never letting go.

Alfie Ju . . .

Julie *composes herself.*

Julie I'd like us to make more of the Garden. D'you remember when we had your Studio constructed the builder was talking about the soil. The moist soil in north London. I did some finding out at the time. But I never did nothing about it. You didn't seem too interested, Alf. It's moist. It suits the Perennials. Himalayan Honeysuckle and Michaelmas Daisy. We could have a little vegetable garden. Cabbage and Cauli. Home-grown stick of celery. Our own compost heap. Rake up the leaves when the season's on the turn.

Alfie I won't see sixty.

Julie You might.

Alfie I won't see seventy.

Julie You will if you want to.

Silence.

Alfie You honestly think two enemas a day, a load of raw carrot juice and a Laetrile infusion will cure me? Do you know what Laetrile is, babe? It breaks down into cyanide. It's more toxic than any chemo I've ever had. That's right. I've had my moments in the middle of the night grasping at straws.

Julie *cries briefly but just as quickly sits on all of it, all the feeling and hurt.*

Alfie Writers don't retire any more than DJs do, do they, babe?

Julie No.

Alfie One day they just stop. Let's not string things out. Don't string it out, let's all say goodbye properly. And then you can leave me to it. In the hospital. Or the hospice. Or wherever I am. I'll be alright.

Julie I won't be.

Alfie I'll have all my memories. And I'll think about you throwing a great big party for me when it's not such a sad time. I can look at my phone.

Julie You can look at your phone?

Alfie As long as I can still pick it up.

Julie It's so selfish, Alfie. It's so fucking selfish.

Alfie I've reached the end of the road, babe . . .

Julie You haven't. Alright. You won't go abroad. But you heard Dr Chan. He said they'd had a big talk about options at the Tumour Board. Mr Rahman said he's happy to go again. If we go down that road. And Dr Chan might get you on a trial.

Alfie But I don't want that, babe.

Julie I don't want you to go.

Alfie This is it, babe. Tell me what you want. What do you want?

Julie I want you home.

Alfie Home?

Julie I want you here.

Julie *looks around the room, thinks.*

Alfie In here?

Julie Yeah.

Alfie In a bed down here?

Alfie *looks around the room, thinks.*

Julie Are you hungry?

Alfie No.

Julie I can mash up a bit of banana and a kiwi fruit with some yoghurt?

Alfie I told you I'm not hungry.

Julie At least let me give you a funeral.

They look at each other for as long as you think you can get away with.

Julie You want that Otis Redding song on the way in?

Alfie I don't know, Ju . . .

Julie And one of your favourites on the way out.

Alfie Maybe.

Julie Can I pick one? Am I allowed?

Alfie You want to pick one?

Julie Yeah. And?

Julie *smiles,* **Alfie** *laughs and offers his phone.*

Julie *goes to* **Alfie** *and takes his phone. She starts to scroll through his iMusic app. She finds the track she's looking for. She looks at* **Alfie**.

Julie You were the first person I ever heard play this record.

Alfie Well I don't know what it is yet?

Julie I was at home with Annabelle. And you had that spot on Centreforce. And Rodney T had just handed over to you. And you were, like. 'Keep it locked London. Here we go. House music all night long.'

Alfie *laughs. 'Your Love' by Frankie Knuckles plays.*

Julie *dances,* **Alfie** *nods his head, enjoying watching her dance. She's a really good dancer, sexy, confident, funny, full of life.*

Julie *realises that it's becoming painful for* **Alfie** *watching her. She stops dancing, and it all becomes much too much for him and he turns away from her. Silence.*

Julie *switches off the music.* **Alfie** *turns back. She goes to him and kisses him, passionately. He lets his hands linger on her bottom.*

Julie *smiles and takes* **Alfie** *by the hand and guides him to the sofa. She takes his walking stick and puts it down.*

Julie *kisses* **Alfie** *and takes his shorts off and has a look at his penis.*

Julie   Going commando I see.

Alfie   Always ready for you, babe.

Julie *laughs, stands and pulls down her knickers which she throws. And then she gently straddles* **Alfie***, kissing him and moving gently against him.*

Alfie *wants to enter her and she helps him and they begin to very gently and beautifully make love. It's been a while and quite quickly he orgasms.*

Julie *holds him,* **Alfie** *holds her. They cling onto each other for dear life. They look at each other for as long as you think you can get away with.*

Julie   You okay?

Alfie   Yeah.

She kisses him, lifts herself off of **Alfie** *and heads over to a box of tissues, before cleaning herself up quickly in the kitchen and washing her hands. Silence.*

Julie *comes back in with some kind of emollient cream. She looks at* **Alfie** *and fetches more tissues.*

Alfie   I want to touch you.

Julie   It's okay.

Alfie   Please.

Julie   I'm gasping for a cup of tea.

Alfie   Thanks a bunch.

Julie   Hold me.

Alfie *nods and* **Julie** *sits next to him on the sofa. They hug, look at each other and* **Julie** *thinks.*

Julie *wipes* **Alfie** *with the tissues and dresses him with the clothes she brought down for him. She uses the emollient cream to soothe his feet and hands.*

She's tender and careful, sensitive to his frailty. She puts the tissues in her pocket. She finds his Sliders.

Alfie Help me up.

Julie Aren't you tired?

Alfie I don't want to sit down. I'll get all locked up.

Julie That tea's gone cold.

Julie *helps* **Alfie** *up. He's a bit unsteady and gestures for his walking stick, which* **Julie** *passes to him. He's in comfortable branded clothes, joggers and a tee-shirt.*

Julie *passes* **Alfie** *his phone, which had fallen out of his pocket on to the sofa. She goes to the teapot and* **Alfie** *watches her.*

Alfie That was the last time wasn't it?

Silence.

Julie It better not be, I didn't get my oats!

Julie *laughs.*

Alfie I think maybe it was.

Julie Don't be daft.

Alfie *laughs and shakes his head.*

Alfie I'm sorry it was so quick . . .

Julie Alf, honestly . . .

Alfie But for me it was lovely. You are lovely. The way you were looking at me . . .

Julie Don't, Alfie, you'll make me cry . . . Annabelle's coming.

Alfie I'm so lucky you didn't walk out on me.

Julie Don't go there. Don't go there. There's no need.

Alfie We'd spent years talking about getting married.

Silence.

Alfie I think I got what I deserved with cancer.

Silence.

Julie What's going on, Alfie? Come on. Our relationship has always been based on complete and total honesty. Apart from the time you fucked your Tour Manager for six months behind my back.

Silence.

Alfie You don't sound like you've ever forgiven me?

Julie Why on earth are you bringing all this up? This is about us now.

Alfie I know. But.

Julie Don't you know how broken I am inside, Alf? This is the last thing I want to talk about now.

Julie *looks for her phone, which she's left charging downstairs overnight. She looks at it briefly and then puts it in her dress pocket.*

Julie *looks at him, thinks.*

Alfie She wants to see me.

Julie What?

Alfie She does. She wants to see me.

Julie Her?

Alfie She heard I'm not well again and she wants to see me.

Julie No.

Alfie That's what I said.

Julie No.

Alfie I felt sick when I saw her email.

Julie She sent you an email did she? Can I see it?

Julie Can I see it, Alf?

Alfie I deleted it, Ju. And I deleted my reply. It made me feel sick.

Julie Is that because you didn't want me to see them?

Alfie I don't want nothing to do with her.

Julie What did you say?

Alfie I told her the past's in the past. I told her you wouldn't want it. I told her not to contact me again.

Julie But is that what you want?

Alfie What?

Julie You told her I wouldn't want you to see her.

Alfie Yeah?

Julie What about you?

Silence.

Julie Well there's my answer.

Alfie I don't, Ju.

Julie This is what all this shit's about.

Alfie It's not.

Julie When did she send you this email?

Alfie Three weeks ago.

Julie Three weeks ago? Three fucking weeks ago and you haven't said shit?

Alfie I knew you'd react.

Julie Well what did you think I was going to do? Hang out the bunting? You shit on me. And if that wasn't enough ten years down the road you've flushed me down the toilet.

Silence.

Julie You think after all these years I don't know you?

Alfie Course I don't.

Julie Is this what all this is about?

Alfie No. Honest. It isn't.

Julie You can't see both of us, you can't have a proper goodbye from both of us, so you won't have none of us.

Alfie My wishes have got nothing to do with her!

Julie Haven't they?

Alfie I don't want nothing to do with her. I've not heard a word from her or seen her in ten years. I don't want to see her. It made me feel like shit.

Julie And now you've made me feel like shit.

Alfie Good riddance to bad rubbish. That's all I am.

Silence.

Julie I don't buy this.

Alfie If you don't believe me have a read. They're in the bin in my old Hotmail.

Alfie *offers* **Julie** *his phone. She hesitates.*

Alfie Go on. Don't you trust me?

Julie I do, Alf. But don't you understand I'll always wonder what she said.

Alfie *offers his phone and* **Julie** *takes it. She finds the emails. It takes the time it takes for her to read them.* **Alfie** *watches her.*

Julie She says here 'I will always love you'. But you don't say nothing about your feelings. Nothing.

Silence.

Julie Did you love her?

Alfie What does it matter?

Julie You told me it was only a shag . . .

Alfie Ju . . .

Julie You did then? You loved her?

Alfie All that matters is we survived. I never, ever stopped loving you. Ever. But do you think I'm the sort of arsehole who'd be in that situation and not feel nothing?

Silence.

Alfie There. Is that better or worse? What good has that done?

Julie There ain't no absolution without the truth first, Alf.

Alfie I was a fool. I didn't say nothing inappropriate. Or false. Or nothing you or me could be ashamed of. Being honest. I did wonder if I'd bump in to her some time. Randomly. At some gig. On the street. In an airport lounge. But when I clicked send. I knew that was it. It's final. This is it. Everything's for the last time now.

Julie *moves towards him, he puts his hands up but she persists and returns his phone.*

Julie *moves away, she hesitates, thinks.*

Julie I've got something to tell you. I need to speak. I need to tell you things. There's things I need to say.

Alfie You can say whatever you want.

Julie Can I?

Alfie Course you can.

Julie I'm frightened as well.

Alfie Of what?

Julie Of how you'll react.

Alfie Just say it, it's okay.

Julie I want to write about us.

Alfie Us?

Julie Yes, us.

Alfie What?

Julie I really thought the Olympics book was going to be the next one . . .

Alfie Right.

Julie But all I can think about is us.

Alfie Right?

Julie And you.

Alfie Me?

Julie And what you're going through . . .

Alfie Right.

Julie And what we're going through and what Annabelle's going through . . . What we're going through as a family.

Alfie Right.

Julie Are you okay?

Alfie I'm fine.

Julie Are you okay for me to tell you this?

Alfie I said, I'm fine.

Julie I'd begun to shape it all in my head like a book . . .

Alfie What?

Julie If I tell myself the story. When it started. The fork in the road. Imagining how it will all turn out in the end. It's a way of reassuring myself I'll get through. Somehow I'll manage.

Silence.

Julie In the last five years. Ever since we first heard the C word out loud. I must have told myself the story of our whole relationship a thousand times in my head. And it's started to organise itself into chapters. One. Nineteen eighty-one. A funny little night club over Hornchurch Bus Garage. Girl meets boy. Two. Two thousand and eleven. Blood. Diagnosis. Three. Back in time. Nineteen eighty-three. DJ Froggy helper. I can't help it. As the months have gone by I've realised I actually. Really. Want to write it. I'm going to write it.

Alfie You wouldn't, would you?

Julie Listen to me.

Alfie Okay.

Julie Nineteen eighty-seven. Our first holiday on The Island. Annabelle was only four wasn't she, Alf? And you went to see Alfredo play and to find out what all the fuss was about.

And you come home at ten o'clock in the morning. Gurning like a goldfish. 'You've got to go Amnesia, Ju, you've got to go, babe'. And the next night you stopped in with Annabel and I went. And I had my first E. And I danced on the terrace until the sun came up. And when I walked back to the apartment I reflected. How brilliant it was you'd had your good time. And then you made sure I could go out and have my good time.

Silence.

Julie The life we've had, Alf. We've done so much. We've been through so much together. Ten years ago you sent an email meant for her to me. And I became a completely different person. Like that.

Julie *clicks her fingers.*

Julie Vengeful, angry. Sometimes consumed by rage.

Alfie Well I never saw that side of you once . . .

Julie I didn't want you to see that me.

Alfie You what?

Julie So I didn't show you. I 'did' instead.

Alfie You did? What did you do, Ju?

Silence.

Julie I told your mum and dad what you'd done.

Alfie You told my mum what I'd done?

Julie nods. *They consider each other.*

Julie I went round to see them. I could see the shame on your dad's face. He sunk back into his armchair. Gripping the arms on it as if he was taking off on an aeroplane.

Alfie What did you do that for?

Julie Your mum made a pot of tea and got the biscuit tin out. She was lovely. It was the only time she was ever nice to me. Though of course she still made it my fault you'd 'dallied'. 'Dallied.' Blaming it on me doing my MA.

Alfie Mum knew?

Julie Yeah, I told them.

Alfie She never said nothing to me about it once.

Julie You was always on a pedestal, Alf.

Alfie Oh my God. What did you do that for?

Silence.

Julie I was hurting bad, Alf. I had an inkling it would never be mentioned again. And once I'd got it off my chest I could try and rebuild myself. And our relationship.

Silence.

Julie I appreciated you stopped touring. I didn't want to seem ungrateful but honestly, Alf . . .

When you was away all the time. I could write at the weekends. I could write after Annabelle went to bed.

When Annabelle was a teenager and went to uni I had even more space. But then you was in my face. And I had another two Karen David books to write. And all the pleasure in writing was gone.

Silence.

Julie It was hard. That time was hard. But we got through it. And we've had a brilliant life together. You still make me laugh.

Silence.

Julie But you see if I don't write it down, Alf. The good and the bad and the indifferent. Everything. It'll all be lost. Everything. Not just you. Everything. You can't leave me on my own without that book.

Alfie Is that why you want to be with me?

Julie What?

Alfie So you can write about me dying.

Julie *composes herself.*

Julie No, that's not fair.

Alfie I'll tell you what's not fair. Knowing you'll never walk your daughter up the aisle on her wedding day. Or play that cheesy old Bros record she loved when she was a kid for her first dance. And come out from behind the decks and lead your partner onto the dancefloor to join her and your son-in-law.

Silence.

Alfie I'll tell you what's not fair. Knowing if your daughter ever has children you'll never watch them bounce up and down on a trampoline in your back garden. That's what's not fair. There. Put that in your fucking book.

Julie Please. Annabelle's coming.

Silence.

Alfie I'm sorry for my anger.

Julie Don't you dare.

Alfie Ju?

Silence.

Julie Why don't I make a fresh pot and why don't we go and have it in the garden?

Alfie I can't be bothered with the garden.

Julie It's such a beautiful morning, Alf...

Alfie I'm tired.

Julie Sit down love.

Alfie If I sit down I won't get back up again.

Julie Why don't you go in The Studio?

Alfie It will make me feel depressed.

Julie Is there football on later?

Alfie I'm not fussed today.

Julie When are England playing again?

Alfie Tomorrow.

Julie Who are we playing?

Alfie Slovakia.

Julie D'you think we'll win?

Alfie Honestly, Julie, I don't know.

Julie I hope he doesn't pick that butterfingers in goal again.

Alfie You don't have to make pointless conversation.

Julie It's not pointless conversation.

Alfie What is it then?

Julie I want you to fight.

Alfie What, fight for more radiotherapy? And chemo? That won't even work.

Julie It might . . .

Alfie And miracle of miracles it does work, surgery that might kill me anyway. And lucky me, if I get through the operation. I'm a bloated husk with a colostomy bag. I want to go with a bit of dignity thanks very much.

Julie But we might get another year?

Alfie Might.

Julie Yes.

Alfie And I might also turn out for Roy Hodgson tomorrow instead of Wayne Rooney.

Silence.

Julie Don't you want to live?

Alfie Of course I want to.

Julie Then try!

Alfie I'm dying, Ju!

Julie Do it for me, do it for Annabelle!

Alfie I'm dying!

Julie Do it for us!

Alfie This is cruel.

Julie How can it be cruel wanting you to live?

Alfie *and* **Julie** *look at each other. They look at each other for as long as you think you can get away with.*

Alfie I've had my time, it's okay.

Julie It's not over . . .

Alfie I've got some regrets . . .

Julie What regrets?

Alfie I wish I'd got sober before I got ill.

Silence.

Alfie I wish I'd taken my own music more seriously. Put more records out.

Silence.

Alfie The things I've seen. In the club. People are ugly, normal, off their heads. You see magical first kisses. Couples breaking up on the dancefloor. I've seen two heart attacks and a stroke. Fella literally died in the club. And we never even switched the music off and put the lights on. There's always one trainspotter standing at the front. You think to yourself. Is he enjoying himself? There's always one angry bloke in the crowd who catches your eye and shows you his middle finger.

Julie There's always one angry bloke . . .

Alfie *laughs, thinks.*

Alfie I keep thinking about that spot I had for a bit at the Berwick. I had a white label of that Joey Beltram record. 'Energy Flash'. As soon as the Berwick hears it they know it's special, right? That hard, nine-o-nine kick. The high hat's driving everything forwards.

Maybe because it was near home. I identified with the kids dancing in front of the booth. Like I used to. Watching Froggy at the Ilford Town Hall Junior Disco every Monday.

Anyway these kids. One of them had a French Crop and he was totally off of his head. And there was another one who had an haircut like Clint Boon. And he was gurning like a motherfucker. And the last one. Was this kid with a classic raver's bob. He was so fresh-faced I don't know how he ever got let in there! They looked fucking funny the three of them. And they caught my eye as I smiled at them and they were having such a great time. Dancing, just dancing. No one was thinking about anything. Except the simple and immense pleasure of the moment.

Silence.

Alfie When that record drops, the pyro goes off, and the smoke's flying through the arms in the air. There's nothing like it. I used to think what I did for a living was trivial. And what you did was important. All those years you spent teaching. Creating books that can last. But I've come round to believing maybe creating fleeting moments of joy in this dark world actually matters.

Silence.

Alfie I've had my time, it's okay. I don't even know if I'd want to be part of the scene now.

Who wants to be on a bill as long as your arm and play an hour-long set? I can't tell a story in an hour. I want it be epic. I want four hours. Five hours. I want to transcend genre. I want to play house, old school, I want to play fresh music, acid, drum and base, northern soul, rare groove, techno, hardcore, disco, garage. I want to play afrobeat one minute and then go bananas with the 'Theme to the Dambusters'. I want to play for people who want to dance and sweat.

Silence.

Alfie But the world's moved on, eh Ju? I'm useless. I'm fucked. But you dancing earlier . . . And I didn't have the strength to join in.

Silence.

Alfie When the time comes. Let me crawl into a corner. Cats have got the right idea. Find a quiet spot on their own and go to sleep.

Julie It's a myth.

Alfie What is?

Julie It's a fairy tale to make us feel better. They're old or sick. Or both. Maybe disoriented and can't find their way back home. They don't know where they are and they're lonely. And they give up. That's all it is.

Alfie Is it?

Julie Alfie, you've got the privilege of musing over the past. Being in the now. You won't be here tomorrow. But I will.

Alfie *nods.*

Alfie I can't do this anymore.

Alfie *gingerly heads into the kitchen out through the back door into the garden. He slams the back door shut as he goes.* **Julie** *is alone. Silence.*

Julie *goes into the kitchen and gets out some plates, bread, ketchup, mayonnaise, HP Sauce, butter and some cutlery, which she brings in and puts on the dining table.*

Julie *notices the teapot. She picks it up and feels it. It's stone cold. She tries to compose herself and closes her eyes.*

She walks in the room. She lets the teapot fall and it smashes on the floor. Broken china and tea go everywhere. She looks at the mess. Silence.

She gets down on her knees and lies on the floor in a foetal position, trying with all her might to keep everything in.

She can't. She screams, voicing all her anguish and pain. Silence.

Alfie *comes back in.* **Julie** *becomes self-conscious and sits up.*

Alfie What's happened here?

They look at the mess, the broken china.

Julie Nana Vi's teapot survived the Blitz, Uncle Peter setting the house in Poole Road on fire during the three-day week and I was hoping it might see off Nigel Farage.

Julie *goes into the kitchen.*

Alfie *looks at the mess. He's upset. She fetches a cloth and a dustpan and brush and begins to clear up.*

Julie I feel like everything's going backwards. The teapot's been another thing.

All the broken china and tea bags go in the bin.

She fetches a bucket of cold water and detergent and washes the floor. It takes the time it takes.

Alfie I don't like to see you like that . . .

Julie What?

Alfie It's as if I can see you here on your own.

Julie *absorbs this and continues cleaning up. She thinks.*

Julie I imagine after the apocalypse we'd have tea. A pot of tea. Me, Annabelle, Toby.

Alfie Tea?

Julie There'd be Gail's sourdough and some custard creams. Maybe we'd open a bottle of white wine. And we'd fall about laughing watching Toby struggle with the cork. Toast your memory.

Julie *gets up, looks at* **Alfie**. *She takes the bucket, cloth and dustpan and brush back into the kitchen.*

Julie *looks at her phone and replies to a WhatsApp. They look at each other, think.*

Julie Annabelle said she'll be another half an hour. Did you go in the Studio?

Alfie No, I was only out there a minute. I fancied a vape.

Julie A vape?

Alfie But Chris next door was giving Tina one. And he'd left the window open.

Julie Oh God.

Alfie It was like he was on the final furlong of the Grand National . . .

Julie You what?

Alfie 'That's it. That's it. Good girl. There's a good girl.'

Julie 'There's a good girl?'

Alfie There am I reflecting upon the meaning of existence. And Chris next door is making me reconsider afresh what it is to make sweet love to a woman.

Silence.

Julie I do want you to consider the options with Dr Chan.

Alfie Ju, babe, please . . .

Julie Alfie, please listen . . . You've got to let me say this . . . You and your dad didn't express no emotions. All you ever did was talk about work, and West Ham and what Annabelle had been up to. I can't imagine how agonising it is, babe. But I promise you it won't be grim. We won't do any howling and crying or anything like that. We'll do what we've always done as a family. Have a laugh. And pull each other's legs.

Alfie But I don't want no more chemo. I can't take any more. I haven't got it in me.

Julie Well we'd make the best of it.

Alfie Well what would we do?

Julie We'd try and get out and about a bit while you've got the energy.

Alfie Where?

Julie We could get down to Rye maybe.

Alfie This is hard.

Julie To Whitstable. Bag of chips. Looking at the sea.

Alfie What else?

Julie We can talk. Talk about anything and everything. We can play Shithead. We can listen to music and reminisce.

Alfie Right.

Julie Maybe if you're feeling up to it we can go to bed. And have a cuddle again.

Silence.

Julie We'll go and vote next Thursday. We'll watch the Euros. Hopefully England will do alright. If you wanted we could go down to have a look at Upton Park before they demolish the stadium. Go in the Pie and Mash on Barking Road. Maybe you could help me with my book?

Alfie What?

Julie Maybe we could do it together . . . It would be something for Annabelle. It would be something for the grandchildren.

Alfie We ain't got no grandchildren.

Silence.

Julie You could tell me what you want. We could talk when you've got the energy. And then when you're resting I would write.

Alfie You do what you like. You hang out all our dirty washing . . .

Julie It hurts you don't trust me, Alf. After everything we've been through. All these years. And I've never let you down once. Not once.

Alfie It's so obvious now it's come to it you've never, ever, forgiven me.

Julie I could have started again. Annabelle had gone to uni.

Alfie I'm sorry, I'm so sorry I did it . . .

Julie I wanted to cut your fucking dick off.

Alfie Well Ju, that's understandable.

Julie Alfie love, I accepted it a long time ago. I decided to put it to the back of my mind as much as I could. A long time ago. Sometimes I thought there was something wrong with me.

Alfie Does Annabelle know? Does she?

Julie She'd never have forgiven us if I'd told her. You, for doing what you did. And me, for telling her.

Silence.

Julie You were the love of my life. You are the love of my life. How could I ever forgive you?

Alfie You're the love of my life.

Julie It's done now. Look at me. It's done.

Silence.

Alfie Why do you want to write about us?

Julie It's okay, I won't do it.

Silence.

Alfie I've read all the stuff in the papers. I know what you've said about your writing. But why would you write about us?

Silence.

Julie When I was a kid I wrote things all the time. I had a secret journal with a padlock. All I did was write down what had happened. Literally. Like when Mum's cat Bobby was run over by the Bin Man. The pleasure I took in describing his crushed hind legs was quite weird. I always wrote stories. But as I got older. It changed. I was a bit ashamed of what I wrote. About my mates, and boys. And Mum and Dad. I wrote down their rows. She didn't think Dad was enough for her.

Silence.

Julie Mum used to find the exercise books I wrote in. And she went absolutely berserk. She ripped them up. She used to scream. 'Don't you think you can write down private things about me and your dad, you little bitch.'

Silence.

Julie I've been writing about my mum my whole life, Alfie babe. Trying to understand her. Where do you think D.I. Karen Davis, the Queen of Romford nick comes from? But I don't literally write my mum.

Silence.

Julie I don't mean to sound callous but I was never much interested in writing about your family. They were so ordinary.

Silence.

Julie I like the feeling when the books come out. I can have an effect on people. It's addictive. After a while I realised I could make people laugh as well. I'm never quick-witted enough in real life. Am I?

Alfie You make me laugh.

Julie I like impressing people. I wasn't a bad teacher but writing . . . When I started to really take it seriously I like impressing you. I like watching you read a manuscript. Pulling a face when something unexpected. Or naughty happens in the story. Don't tell me that's never going to happen again.

Julie *wants to cry. Doesn't.*

Alfie Do I deserve you? Have I ever deserved you?

He walks in the room.

Alfie Tell the truth in your book. I don't want no hogwash. I don't want people thinking I was some beige wanker.

Julie People don't think you're beige, babe. They've only got to go on YouTube. That video of you at Raindance is really something quite special.

Alfie That is thirty seconds of infamy that is.

Julie It is.

Alfie That's a one-man advert that is. For why it's not good to consume a gram of Charlie, six Doves and a Purple Ohm.

Julie *laughs.* **Alfie** *laughs. Silence.*

Alfie You know everything. You can write a perfect book.

Julie I don't know about that.

Alfie Will you help me talk to Annabelle?

Julie Annabelle's pregnant.

Alfie What?

Julie You know. Pregnant.

Julie *makes a pregnant belly gesture and smiles.*

Alfie She's what?

Julie She did the test last week.

Alfie What?

Julie I think she did about three. One after the other.

Alfie She's pregnant?

Julie Yeah.

Alfie Why didn't you tell me? Did Annabelle ask you not to tell me?

Silence.

Julie The baby's due beginning-middle of February.

Alfie *lets his walking stick fall. They look at the walking stick.*

Alfie I'm alright, Ju. It's lovely news. I'm over the moon.

Alfie *looks at his walking stick and gingerly gets down on one knee to pick it up.*

Julie *goes to him and helps him back up.*

Julie It's okay.

Alfie I'm alright, I'm alright.

Julie You don't have to be.

Alfie Well I'll know to rearrange my face when she tells me.

Silence.

Alfie Annabelle, blimey, out of wedlock.

Julie Didn't have Annabelle up the duff on my Annabelle bingo card. Did you?

Alfie No.

Silence.

Julie I loved those summers on The Island.

Alfie When Annabelle was little?

Julie Yeah.

Alfie Me too.

Julie That rave in Slough?

Alfie Yeah.

Julie You were on the back of that flat bed truck with the sound system with Danny. And he played that Sergio Mendes record. And Annabelle. Was holding on to your leg and laughing. The floor was moving about so much.

Alfie What are you going to do when I'm gone? What are you really going to do?

Julie I don't want to talk about it, Alf babe.

Alfie Annabelle will need help, won't she? She'll need help with the baby. When the baby comes. Won't she, Ju?

Julie I don't want to talk about it now.

Silence.

Alfie You need to get on with your life, Julie.

Julie I honestly don't know.

Alfie You should get yourself on a cruise. The ones they do for single people.

Julie Alf . . .

Alfie Just be careful. Two weeks in the Caribbean on the Azura and that's a lot of silver surfers with a touch of the itchy ball sack.

Julie *laughs*. **Alfie** *laughs*.

Julie The idea of another body is . . .

Alfie Probably quite appealing.

Julie You couldn't be more wrong. I've only ever wanted you.

Alfie You could get yourself a dog. It will be some company. See your mates. Do things you enjoy. Go out dancing.

Julie I'm too old to go out dancing.

Alfie Drop a couple of Benny's. Bosh. Have it. You're a fantastic dancer.

Julie I don't want you to go.

Alfie You'll be alright. You will. Everything will be alright in the end.

Julie The only certainty I've got is Annabelle. And my work.

Alfie What do you imagine? What's in your head? What's your day like?

Julie I can't Alf . . .

Alfie Go on. You can do it.

Julie Erm. Listening to Radio Four in the morning. *The Today Programme*. Tea and toast with marmalade in bed. The house is quiet. A walk. To clear my head and think about the book. Maybe a loop of Ally Pally. Or a walk over to Crouch End. One day over the railway track at Harringay. The next day over Hornsey. Perhaps a coffee in Gail's with my notebook. Gawp at all the Crouch End types. And ear-wig their pretensions. And fail completely to acknowledge I am one of them. And have been for a long time.

Alfie You know what you could do, Ju?

Julie What?

Alfie You could turn the Studio into your office.

Julie I couldn't do that . . .

Alfie It's yours.

Julie I couldn't . . .

Alfie I want you to.

Julie What am I going to with all your vinyl?

Alfie See what Annabelle wants. And sell the rest.

Julie To who?

Alfie There'll be a hundred and one vinyl junkies all over it. You won't have no trouble.

Julie It's too hard after everything . . .

Alfie It's not. You're strong. You're the strongest person I know.

Julie Am I?

Alfie You can write in the Studio. Put a wood burner in there. A dog basket under your desk. For the puppy. In the summer work with the doors open. Like I did.

Julie Could I?

Alfie All your writer mates will be well jealous. You'll have the biggest shed of the lot.

They look at each other for as long as you think you can get away with.

Julie Now you know about Annabelle, are you sure, Alf?

Silence.

Julie You don't have to decide anything now.

Silence.

Julie But you might feel different when you wake up tomorrow? You might feel different after you've seen Annabelle? Don't you think Annabelle might want to be with you?

Especially now what with her news.

Alfie *feels agitated and walks in the room a touch.*

Julie She's going to be devastated when we tell her you don't want no more treatment. But if we can tell her that we're looking at options. Perhaps February's unrealistic . . . But perhaps. Perhaps. If you could experience feeling the baby kick in Annabelle's tummy. Put your hands on Annabelle's tummy. And Annabelle could experience that.

Alfie *wipes a few tears away from his eyes.*

Julie Remember when Annabelle kicked and you loved it? When you could sometimes see the ripple on my tummy when she moved. Annabelle was a proper night-time raver wasn't she? Just like her dad.

Alfie *nods, wipes his eyes and composes himself. He looks at* **Julie***.*

Alfie I'm sorry about my egregious, misplaced and erroneous cat analogy.

Julie What about your egregious, misplaced and erroneous cat analogy?

Alfie I feel like a bit of a berk.

Julie A bit of a berk?

Alfie A wally.

Julie A wally?

Alfie A monumental and major wally. I feel like it's the last night of Space. The closing fiesta. And it's me and Carl. And Carl can't find that Angie Stone record he loves. It's perfect. It's the perfect record to close out the season. But he can't find it.

Alfie *sings a bit of the melody.*

Alfie So he's like 'you play the last one, Alf'. And I'm like, hang on, Carl, hang on, mate. And he's like 'What?' And I'm like I've played all my records. There's nothing left in the box. And he's like 'you must have something, what's that?' And I'm like, that's a Max Bygraves . . .

Julie A what?

Alfie 'You're a pink toothbrush, I'm a blue toothbrush.'

Julie *laughs.*

Alfie But it's all I've got left in the box. It's my anxiety dream.

Julie That's your anxiety dream?

Alfie I clear the dancefloor and everyone hates me.

Julie No one hates you.

Alfie No?

Julie No one will hate you.

Alfie No?

Julie I love you. Of course I'll do what you want. If what you've said. It's how you want things to be at the end. Then I respect your wishes. Of course I do, babe.

Silence.

Alfie You know Space is closing permanently at the end of the season? End of an era that is.

Julie Space going at the end of the summer. Upton Park gone. It makes you wonder what else is around the corner, don't it, Alfie babe?

Alfie *thinks, tries to hold himself together.*

Alfie I don't want to die.

Julie I don't want you to die.

Alfie I love you.

Julie I love you more.

Alfie I love you more.

Julie Dickhead.

Alfie Twat.

Julie Fucking dickhead.

They look at each other for as long as you think you can get away with.

Alfie Maybe I can think about doing things a bit differently.

Julie It's your life.

Alfie It's not, it's our life.

Julie I think it is. It's your life and its precious. Don't you dare change your mind. Don't you dare.

Alfie When Annabelle comes we'll tell her I'm having some more Chemo.

Julie Will you?

Alfie Buy a bit more time. We'll tell her. We'll tell her whatever happens we'll all be together. Funny stories and pulling each other's legs.

Julie Do you really mean it, Alf?

Alfie Yeah, yeah, I do.

Julie What is it, love?

Alfie I hate cancer. I hate cancer more than I hate Millwall.

They look at each other.

Alfie *makes a decision. He goes to* **Julie** *and gets down on one knee.*

Julie Alf . . .

Alfie I'm sorry I'm a dickhead.

Julie Please babe, you've said sorry you don't have to do this any more . . . You're forgiven. I forgive you. I forgive you.

Alfie But will you marry me?

Julie What?

Alfie Will you marry me?

Julie *has a look around the room.*

Julie What?

Alfie It has been. It is. The greatest honour and privilege that you let me share my life with you. I love you with all my heart. And for always. I love you. If there's still time, will you marry me?

They look at each other for as long as you think you can get away with.

Julie No. We're alright as we are.

Alfie No?

Julie No.

Alfie What?

Julie Had you going there . . .

Alfie Where?

Julie Babe, joke. Joke, babe.

Alfie Oh.

Julie *laughs.* **Alfie** *laughs.*

Julie *gets down on her knees and hugs him and kisses him. They look at each other.*

Julie Of course I will. I love you.

Alfie Thank you, I love you.

They kiss. Julie's phone starts to ring in the kitchen. She gets up and goes and gets it.

Julie Hello babe, hello . . .

She comes back in.

It's Annabelle.

Alfie Ju . . .

Julie She's two minutes away.

Alfie For Christ's sake tell her to get off the phone . . .

Julie She's on the car speakerphone.

Julie *listens.* **Alfie** *feels uncomfortable but she's focused on Annabelle.*

Julie Alf, Toby's only got himself a shiner . . .

Alfie What?

Julie Went to see 'a show' in a funny little cabaret club with his mates. And the performer shot a mini vibrator out of her vagina. And bop. Copped it smack in the face.

She laughs.

Poor Toby . . .

Alfie Ju!

Julie Yes, I'll get the bacon on now. Yes, I know you like it crispy.

Julie *looks at* **Alfie** *and smiles.*

Julie Here, Annabelle, you'll never guess what? Your dad's just asked me to marry him.

She briefly holds the phone away from her ear.

I know. Better late than never. The old romantic's still down on one knee.

Alfie That's because I can't fucking get up.

Julie Oh . . . Listen babe, I'll see you in a minute.

She listens.

Listen, babe, we'll chat when you get here . . .

She listens, glances at **Alfie**.

Julie   Thank you. Thank you. Yeah, we're over the moon.

She ends the call and puts the phone in her pocket. She goes to **Alfie** *and helps him up.*

Alfie   Is she pleased?

Julie   Very.

Alfie   Are you?

Julie   I am.

Alfie   Will you help me talk to her? Will you help me explain I won't get better? All I've got is a bit more time.

They absorb this. Silence.

Julie   She said 'are you getting married because there's really bad news?'

Alfie   Did she?

Julie   Are we?

Alfie   At the end of the night. You play the best record in your box.

Julie   I think so.

Alfie *looks around the room. Thinks about what lies ahead.*

Julie *nods and goes into the kitchen. She gets a frying pan out and on the hob.*

She takes the oil and gets some in the pan and takes the bacon from the fridge. She begins to heat the oil.

Alfie *takes his phone out and looks for something. He finds the song and presses play. 'Promised Land' by Joe Smooth plays.*

He can smell the bacon cooking. The doorbell goes. **Alfie** *turns off the music.* **Julie** *comes in from the kitchen.*

Silence.

Julie She'll be alright.

Alfie Will she?

Julie We'll tell her. We'll tell her we want a good end. And that's exactly what we're going to have.

The doorbell goes again. They look at each other for as long as you think you can get away with.

The doorbell goes again. **Julie**'s *phone starts to ring. They ignore it.*

Julie *goes to* **Alfie** *hugs him and kisses him and then heads out.* **Alfie** *composes himself, finds some courage and puts a smile on his face.*

End.

Discover. Read. Listen. Watch.

A NEW WAY TO ENGAGE WITH PLAYS

This award-winning digital library features over 3,000 playtexts, 400 audio plays, 300 hours of video and 360 scholarly books.

Playtexts published by Methuen Drama, The Arden Shakespeare, Faber & Faber, Playwrights Canada Press, Aurora Metro Books and Nick Hern Books.

Audio Plays from L.A. Theatre Works featuring classic and modern works from the oeuvres of leading American playwrights.

Video collections including films of live performances from the RSC, The Globe and The National Theatre, as well as acting masterclasses and BBC feature films and documentaries.

FIND OUT MORE:
www.dramaonlinelibrary.com • @dramaonlinelib

Methuen Drama Modern Plays

include

Bola Agbaje
Edward Albee
Ayad Akhtar
Jean Anouilh
John Arden
Peter Barnes
Sebastian Barry
Clare Barron
Alistair Beaton
Brendan Behan
Edward Bond
William Boyd
Bertolt Brecht
Howard Brenton
Amelia Bullmore
Anthony Burgess
Leo Butler
Jim Cartwright
Lolita Chakrabarti
Caryl Churchill
Lucinda Coxon
Tim Crouch
Shelagh Delaney
Ishy Din
Claire Dowie
David Edgar
David Eldridge
Dario Fo
Michael Frayn
John Godber
James Graham
David Greig
John Guare
Lauren Gunderson
Peter Handke
David Harrower
Jonathan Harvey
Robert Holman
David Ireland
Sarah Kane
Barrie Keeffe
Jasmine Lee-Jones
Anders Lustgarten
Duncan Macmillan
David Mamet
Patrick Marber
Martin McDonagh
Arthur Miller
Alistair McDowall
Tom Murphy
Phyllis Nagy
Anthony Neilson
Peter Nichols
Ben Okri
Joe Orton
Vinay Patel
Joe Penhall
Luigi Pirandello
Stephen Poliakoff
Lucy Prebble
Peter Quilter
Mark Ravenhill
Philip Ridley
Willy Russell
Jackie Sibblies Drury
Sam Shepard
Martin Sherman
Chris Shinn
Wole Soyinka
Simon Stephens
Kae Tempest
Anne Washburn
Laura Wade
Theatre Workshop
Timberlake Wertenbaker
Roy Williams
Snoo Wilson
Frances Ya-Chu Cowhig
Benjamin Zephaniah

Methuen Drama Contemporary Dramatists

include

John Arden (two volumes)
Arden & D'Arcy
Peter Barnes (three volumes)
Sebastian Barry
Mike Bartlett
Clare Barron
Brad Birch
Dermot Bolger
Edward Bond (ten volumes)
Howard Brenton (two volumes)
Leo Butler (two volumes)
Richard Cameron
Jim Cartwright
Caryl Churchill (two volumes)
Complicite
Sarah Daniels (two volumes)
Nick Darke
David Edgar (three volumes)
David Eldridge (two volumes)
Ben Elton
Per Olov Enquist
Dario Fo (two volumes)
Michael Frayn (four volumes)
John Godber (four volumes)
Paul Godfrey
James Graham (two volumes)
David Greig
John Guare
Lee Hall (two volumes)
Katori Hall
Peter Handke
Jonathan Harvey (two volumes)
Iain Heggie
Israel Horovitz
Declan Hughes
Terry Johnson (three volumes)
Sarah Kane
Barrie Keeffe
Bernard-Marie Koltès (two volumes)
Franz Xaver Kroetz
Kwame Kwei-Armah
David Lan
Bryony Lavery
Deborah Levy
Doug Lucie

Alistair MacDowall
Sabrina Mahfouz
David Mamet (six volumes)
Patrick Marber
Martin McDonagh
Duncan McLean
David Mercer (two volumes)
Anthony Minghella (two volumes)
Rory Mullarkey
Tom Murphy (six volumes)
Phyllis Nagy
Anthony Neilson (three volumes)
Peter Nichol (two volumes)
Philip Osment
Gary Owen
Louise Page
Stewart Parker (two volumes)
Joe Penhall (two volumes)
Stephen Poliakoff (three volumes)
David Rabe (two volumes)
Mark Ravenhill (three volumes)
Christina Reid
Philip Ridley (two volumes)
Willy Russell
Eric-Emmanuel Schmitt
Ntozake Shange
Sam Shepard (two volumes)
Martin Sherman (two volumes)
Christopher Shinn (two volumes)
Joshua Sobel
Wole Soyinka (two volumes)
Simon Stephens (five volumes)
Shelagh Stephenson
David Storey (three volumes)
C. P. Taylor
Sue Townsend
Judy Upton (two volumes)
Michel Vinaver (two volumes)
Arnold Wesker (two volumes)
Peter Whelan
Michael Wilcox
Roy Williams (four volumes)
David Williamson
Snoo Wilson (two volumes)
David Wood (two volumes)
Victoria Wood

Methuen Drama Student Editions

Alan Ayckbourn *Confusions* • **Mike Bartlett** *Earthquakes in London* • **Aphra Behn** *The Rover* • **Alice Birch** *Revolt. She Said. Revolt Again* • **Edward Bond** *Lear* • *Saved* • **Bertolt Brecht** *The Caucasian Chalk Circle* • *Fear and Misery in the Third Reich* • *The Good Person of Szechwan* • *Life of Galileo* • *Mother Courage and her Children* • *The Resistible Rise of Arturo Ui* • *The Threepenny Opera* • **Jon Brittain** *Rotterdam* • **Georg Büchner** *Woyzeck* • **Anton Chekhov** *The Cherry Orchard* • *The Seagull* • *Three Sisters* • *Uncle Vanya* • **Caryl Churchill** *Serious Money* • *Top Girls* • **Shelagh Delaney** *A Taste of Honey* • **Inua Ellams** *Barber Shop Chronicles* • **Euripides** *Elektra* • *Medea* • **Dario Fo** *Accidental Death of an Anarchist* • **Michael Frayn** *Copenhagen* • **John Galsworthy** *Strife* • **Nikolai Gogol** *The Government Inspector* • **Carlo Goldoni** *A Servant to Two Masters* • **James Graham** *This House* • **Tanika Gupta** *The Empress* • **Katori Hall** *The Mountaintop* • **Lorraine Hansberry** *A Raisin in the Sun* • **Robert Holman** *Across Oka* • **Henrik Ibsen** *A Doll's House* • *Ghosts* • *Hedda Gabler* • **Sarah Kane** *4.48 Psychosis* • *Blasted* • **Charlotte Keatley** *My Mother Said I Never Should* • **Dennis Kelly** *DNA* • **Bernard Kops** *Dreams of Anne Frank* • **Federico García Lorca** *Blood Wedding* • *Doña Rosita the Spinster* (bilingual edition) • *The House of Bernarda Alba* (bilingual edition) • *Yerma* (bilingual edition) • **David Mamet** *Glengarry Glen Ross* • *Oleanna* • **Patrick Marber** *Closer* • **John Marston** *The Malcontent* • **Martin McDonagh** *The Lieutenant of Inishmore* • *The Lonesome West* • *The Beauty Queen of Leenane* • *The Cripple of Inishmaan* • **Alistair McDowall** *Pomona* • **John McGrath** *The Cheviot, the Stag and the Black, Black Oil* • **Arthur Miller** *All My Sons* • *The Crucible* • *A View from the Bridge* • *Death of a Salesman* • *The Price* • *After the Fall* • *The Last Yankee* • *A Memory of Two Mondays* • *Broken Glass* • *Incident at Vichy* • *The American Clock* • *The Ride Down Mt. Morgan* • **Joe Orton** *Loot* • **Joe Penhall** *Blue/Orange* • **Luigi Pirandello** *Six Characters in Search of an Author* • **Lucy Prebble** *Enron* • **Mark Ravenhill** *Shopping and F***ing* • **Reginald Rose** *Twelve Angry Men* • **Willy Russell** *Blood Brothers* • *Educating Rita* • **Lemn Sissay** Benjamin Zephaniah's *Refugee Boy* • **Sophocles** *Antigone* • *Oedipus the King* • **Wole Soyinka** *Death and the King's Horseman* • **Simon Stephens** *Punk Rock* • *Pornography* • **Shelagh Stephenson** *The Memory of Water* • **August Strindberg** *Miss Julie* • **J. M. Synge** *The Playboy of the Western World* • **Kae Tempest** *Wasted* • **Theatre Workshop** *Oh What a Lovely War* • **Laura Wade** *Posh* • **Frank Wedekind** *Spring Awakening* • **Timberlake Wertenbaker** *Our Country's Good* • **Arnold Wesker** *The Merchant* • **Peter Whelan** *The Accrington Pals* • **Oscar Wilde** *The Importance of Being Earnest* • **Roy Williams** *Sing Yer Heart Out for the Lads* • **Tennessee Williams** *A Streetcar Named Desire* • *The Glass Menagerie* • *Cat on a Hot Tin Roof* • *Sweet Bird of Youth*

Methuen Drama World Classics
include

Jean Anouilh (two volumes)
John Arden (two volumes)
Brendan Behan
Aphra Behn
Bertolt Brecht (eight volumes)
Georg Büchner
Mikhail Bulgakov
Pedro Calderón
Karel Čapek
Peter Nichols (two volumes)
Anton Chekhov
Noël Coward (nine volumes)
Georges Feydeau (two volumes)
Eduardo De Filippo
Max Frisch (two volumes)
John Galsworthy
Nikolai Gogol (two volumes)
Maxim Gorky (two volumes)
Harley Granville Barker
(two volumes)
Victor Hugo
Henrik Ibsen (six volumes)
Alfred Jarry
Federico García Lorca
(three volumes)
Pierre Marivaux
Mustapha Matura
David Mercer
(two volumes)
Arthur Miller (six volumes)
Molière
Pierre de Musset
Joe Orton
A. W. Pinero
Luigi Pirandello
Terence Rattigan
W. Somerset Maugham
August Strindberg
(three volumes)
J. M. Synge
Ramón del Valle-Inclán
Frank Wedekind
Oscar Wilde
Tennessee Williams

Methuen Drama
Classical Greek Dramatists

Aeschylus Plays: One
(Persians, Seven Against Thebes, Suppliants,
Prometheus Bound)

Aeschylus Plays: Two
(Oresteia: Agamemnon, Libation-Bearers, Eumenides)

Aristophanes Plays: One
(Acharnians, Knights, Peace, Lysistrata)

Aristophanes Plays: Two
(Wasps, Clouds, Birds, Festival Time, Frogs)

Aristophanes & Menander: New Comedy
(Women in Power, Wealth, The Malcontent,
The Woman from Samos)

Euripides Plays: One
(Medea, The Phoenician Women, Bacchae)

Euripides Plays: Two
(Hecuba, The Women of Troy, Iphigeneia at Aulis, Cyclops)

Euripides Plays: Three
(Alkestis, Helen, Ion)

Euripides Plays: Four
(Elektra, Orestes, Iphigeneia in Tauris)

Euripides Plays: Five
(Andromache, Herakles' Children, Herakles)

Euripides Plays: Six
(Hippolytos, Suppliants, Rhesos)

Sophocles Plays: One
(Oedipus the King, Oedipus at Colonus, Antigone)

Sophocles Plays: Two
(Ajax, Women of Trachis, Electra, Philoctetes)

For a complete listing of
Methuen Drama titles, visit:
www.bloomsbury.com/drama

Follow us on Twitter and keep up to date
with our news and publications
@MethuenDrama